Ash Grove

Poems

by

William LaPage

Finishing Line Press
Georgetown, Kentucky

Ash Grove

Poems

ACKNOWLEDGMENTS

I would like to thank the editors of the following journals in which early
versions of these poems first appeared:

The Awakenings Review: "Ghost Story"
The Bangalore Review: "Candela"
New Note Poetry: "Estranged"
The Rockvale Review: "Mission Station"

I would also like to thank my parents and sister for their love, support,
and encouragement. I want to thank Sara Burge, Marcus Cafagña, Jennifer
Murvin, Michael Czyzniejewski and the Creative Writing faculty at Missouri
State University, Shane Seely, John Dalton, Andrea Scarpino, Danielle
Beirne, Kerry James Evans, Poetry in the Woods, the Creative Writing
faculty at University of Missouri—St. Louis, Bill and Joyce Pyle, Gwyn
Knauer, William Espinet III, Crystal Lane. Above all, I want to thank my
partner, Hailey Pedersen, without whom this book would not be possible.

Publisher: Leah Huete de Maines
Editor: Christen Kincaid
Cover Art: Danielle Beirne
Author Photo: Hailey Pedersen
Cover Design: Elizabeth Maines McCleavy

Order online: www.finishinglinepress.com
also available on amazon.com

Author inquiries and mail orders:
Finishing Line Press
PO Box 1626
Georgetown, Kentucky 40324
USA

Contents

for my parents

1°

By degrees
the flood waters loosen
the furniture's grip, careening
stump and stool center the room
in the house's staggered dark.
Unfinished objects lost in translation
lost in thought sharpen
on razor-thin moonlight
that cuts through them
at night when they pretend to sleep.
        A one-degree difference
is all the difference needed
to sour the air, flex the porch screen
tight like a sail
sailing them into late summer rhythms
from which the pavement cedes
twilight pools streetlight spins glittering
across the aluminum rooftops.
        On the wall
the window is the last to go, contains
in it a view of the neighbor's lily garden.
Its shade races the pond underwater
to reach sunset shimmers
over lily pedestals entranced
in their lame poses. The empty pipes
inside the now dark fountain
moan beyond sleep. When I stay
the night throws off its balance.
I want there to be a moral at the end.

Estranged

From every blood vein runs through
the city, dulled in tumblers of tedium,
mirrored in windows on sidestreets,
the familiar birdsong of nailgun chatter,
of roofers in a race against the sun,
I am taking the long walk around,
penitent, hands pitched in empty pockets.
There is more than we might want to know,
about the commotion in a stairwell that simmers,
like echolocation, cautions us from a distance.
The pneumatic hisses quiet, freeway traffic
comes to a halt. An accident rushes over
every surface, almost imperceptible,
horns ricochet off the trolley bridge,
its oxidized glyphs recall forgotten names,
counting down the number of days left
in summer. These mercies reach beyond,
woven through the ironworks. Heat siphons
the air from the street, burns up the oxygen.
In the alley the estranged paw the leeways
where they scavenge leftovers
in the act of starving their hunger.

Ghost Story

When the TV turns to static,
and the evening has gotten away from us,
when the dishes are left to stew in the sink overnight,
consider how the children would be too young to be up
so late, watching movies, a sitter somewhere unawares.
There was something I meant to share with you,
some pearl, some antique adage I read
in a pamphlet from the doctor's waiting room.
Consider the children, in their beds, frightened
of a gnarled oak while outside their bedroom window
lightning flashes crystalline auras across the closet door.
Consider how some disturbance wakes us, like
a radio alarm tuning without agency,
like a backfire cracking the night wide open, or
the neighbor's newborn crying, brings us close
to the rim of waking life, far from the diagnosis
of waking-dreams that sound like, look like,
feel like cold displacement in the dark.
Consider the children, when they're old enough,
how we might explain it like a brainstorm, like
an electromagnetic impulse, a freak misfire,
like two tangential brains discordant.
Not the thunderclap outside, but the lightning
calling from inside your head.
Consider the past is all *c'est la vie.*
Consider memory is an ancient burial ground for language.
The way we drown in our love.
The way we pull each other under fighting to rescue the other.
How butterscotch-sweet fear is going down.
How it's like being eaten alive by an oak,
but also like swimming in a pool of skeletons.
Consider the ceiling is a black portal full of voices
we stared into the night you dropped the glass in the sink.
How the last major episode was years ago.
How the long estrangement after still haunts us.
What would happen to the children ten years from now?
A lifetime extracting blood samples to test liver enzymes.

Upping and downing. Milligrams and microdoses.
Consider the mind is a noisy ghost of distractions.
The homunculus run amok.
A conditional *déjà vu*, if-then equation:
if only we could sleep a full night,
if only it was the alarm, if only there were words
to explain how this works, and I could remember
what I forgot, we could settle if settling is what we wanted.
Take solace in the quiet. Maybe then have children
who stay up past their bedtime watching movies.

Mission Station

I remember when we were first cut
in the island's off season from
the hotel bars, after all the drinks
we could afford, so long as we stayed in back
and didn't trouble the waitress, so long
as we paid cash and left by the backdoor.
We closed the place out in the foreglow
morning overcast, stumbled over the broken
palmetto fronds, rebels fashioned
patently in sunglasses. Hotel-hopping
we never slept in the same suite twice,
or we camped on the dunes
under a rain-scented umbrella orphaned
by the wind when the deposit on the room
over the bodega ran out. Our futures were remote
as what we equated with the pumpjack fields
sawing the horizon to dust, fields of supplicants
to their recompense. And far ahead we watched
the miles-long train trace and vanish
into the winecolored daubs of the river valley.
So we go because our going is boundless, because
I remember when the peppertrees blossomed,
late as August, along the two-lane blacktop,
past the mainland dwellings, broken bottle glass
tarred atop their walls, fine as razors,
desolate as the bus ride back to the Mission.

Silver Springs

With the same surety as she passes
through the park, the train is already
barreling through town, like a
spring-fed scar tracked across the naked arms
of alley walls, a procession
in grave-black steelcars advances
slow on coal-tarred rails. It's apparition
of graffitied light appeals to the tunnel it cuts
hawked high with the ruins of hollowed out nights.
Its lamp bores a hole through 2AM
windows of warrens and switchhouses
where the watchman watches the lights
of the feedmill and the distances
recede from the river. Years later
I came to recognize the teared pearl
of her face from the spyglass of my neighbor's house
watching out from her kitchen perch,
small world or small town,
we pulled her son's body off the tracks.
Deep night the park falls into cave echoes
choirs of cicadas make
granting wishes harvested from smoke
flames whittle to glass shards.
She didn't know what she wanted except
for the world to stop. She counts
the molten cinders that spark and pinwheel
across the pitch and tarsand calling her,
tempting and unstoppable.

Winter Solstice

At night near the park
the catalpa clings to
escarpment,
to veins of shellrock
weathered for an
epoch, the gnarled
knob of its body,
disbands
in gold bedrock and
shoulders the burden
as time
passes,
just by you,
its skin pale green
and hairier
as if heavier
and darker
after rain. We
did not see it then
passing for a game
once we were old enough
to drive
and drove by looking
for the ghost—
a play of angled streetlight
and graffiti. As if passing now
the eves claim the hollow bells
brittled from how burned
sediment set aflame
reddened the southern sky
a low shade copper,
and the limestone
cavities
and limbs cut free
by the wind
fall along
the side of the road
as we pass
no different.

Ash Grove

1.

Passing under the archways
of their interlocked veins
and the shaded tangle in asymmetries
bows the canopy of the ash grove
toward blessings over the traveler's road.
Like a mourning chorus in winter
cars idle along our avenue cracked
and potholed and weathered avenue,
the trees in their estrangement crane
together in the tethers the way they
stand sentry and no one notices
the frays of the kite string
wound round their winter branches
tarred the whole grove together.

Wild cords break and bud too early for spring
and dry out and the wickered mosses
draw a frame over the thatched towers
of the grove keeper's vacancy.
Pinlets of light rattle in his eyes,
needling through the dark curtain, through
the pale glint of its unmended horizon,
where the sky comes down low
and the footpath stained with resin.
Under the rustle of ash branches
in fall chill squirrels knuckle
the popped walnut on the pavement
who maintains in its body record
a memory, old as the wind.

2.

Ashchips covered the dirt floor
of their one-room shantyhouse. They were
carpeted in the same moss green, and as cold
to touch, but with a stench of mildew.
Not dank or brackish earth scents
but slightly tangy-dank smoke stained
with a hint of wet fur. Under this earthen blanket
his albescent bones seed and take root.
The boy sat in the front room as if perched
on his high stool, conducting as if
once, there was a door leading out,
past the pasture beyond,
where the only shelter nature provided
was a space where the boy could crawl into
when the sheriff came looking.
On all sides at distance of five feet by five feet
walls carved by hand, the house seemed
though no one knew why
to have been the first place
the small family settled.
The white walls around which so affected
the inside and outside of the woods
weren't much different from the boy's
own marbled skin, though
When he was big enough
he could take down a sapling
with his fist if he so chose.
All this the boy did
before he followed the footpath
from the house and into the grove.

3.

After felling the ash registered
no change in its condition
from being wild in nature
to being a part of a construct the animate
mobile creatures had fashioned
into kindling it served to fire,
the grove in fact held no opinion
of the world. Children would look
up at the spires and think they felt something
in the way the trees swayed but didn't move.
There was no evidence it did.
The trees were there, and one day
the boy cleaved one trunk and found
hidden inside its body a squirrel's nest.

And standing under the ashes looking up
he felt time move away from him,
one field to another, its rolling carrying him away.
Of those who came around to the Ash Grove,
those who searched under her shade in summer
or who came to the house looking for mom
while he was out collecting for the fire
saw from the road at a distance
the shanty was hardly more than a flicker.
He left his wild life, wild in itself
wild in his own way, being
part of the wild, neglected and almost feral.
Without his knowing arrangements
had already been made
by a cousin or maid who took to harvesting
him from the earth, in carrying him away.
The next day he was gone, the nest
scattered some distance away by the wind.

4.

That was only one time the boy escaped.
Over time the path wore down
and there were many more homes.
What happened to the Ash Grove
in his absence did not very much effect
his main disposition, he learned.
Most who rode the boxcars
or even for those who wished to
who raced as it gathered speed,
its main attraction that it would
take you away from one city to another.
Oh, people fell who faltered the jump
off the car, but that was never due
to any fault of their going. They fell because
one was suddenly ill or stumbled or often
they were too drunk or even sometimes
because they were pushed. Most everyone
who came to the camp was welcomed
at all time by whomever happened
to wear the crown of coalash. Back then
the Ash Grove was barely a switchyard bar and yet
the boy had been seriously hurt leaping there.

5.

Once, the tracks led to a house larger
than he ever knew, two bedrooms upstairs
and a large living room, even a dining room
downstairs, the kitchen remodeled,
built a long time ago when the city
was younger, rented to a father, a mother,
their two newborns. One child was an engineer,
followed her father as he spun out his days.
The mother goes into different rooms all day
and all her clothes are clean and pleated.
Often the father stares out the window
at the sapling in the front yard. The son
stands leaning against its mast looking up
on the life of a man and a nature promised
beyond the house he sees. The father
will sometimes stand under the tree
looking up at the son climbing,
holding the spot steady, flicking the ash
from the end of his cigarette.

6.

Before he was old enough, all paths
led to his mother's tap hall,
to the stairwell with its apartment upstairs.
The Ash Grove is decorated in basal, silver,
all polished brass rails. No one sits in the room
but the boy, alone. Everyone is playing
in the hall. The apartment is rotted, empty,
is being demolished many decades later,
to the crash of boxcars coupling nearby.
The noise they make skirting
sweeps through the grove. Cars kick up
concrete dust everywhere, making one onlooker
think: *I would like to get away from this;*
I'll go to the desert where there is only ash.
A man in a blue hat tells the boy:
It is foolish to waste your time.
The boy is taken in and sold for a small sum
to a family who arranges performances
at the church. Before, leading to the sanctuary,
he had only rotting floor planks.
A boy is a strange thing to buy, he thinks,
he tells the story when the children are older.
Now there is tuning in the choir pit, he says.
When the sermon is ended, the people
go out into the parking lot. In the air
they are for a moment their lost thoughts
about all the mercies they heard
but don't believe.

7.

Now, the night invents streets and alleys
and one leads to another far away
city buildings and parks and cypress swaying
against an azure, blood and sulfur-colored sky.
On the boy's head appears stars for a crown.
His feet are cumulonimbus white.
When the heat storms come they wash
away his soles, thundering, from a universe within
and washes him away.
                              When someone asks
which path through the ash grove
leads into memory, the boy says, *all*.
Nothing more than made up.
There was no green rug of moss.
It had eroded by the time they arrived.
There was no Ash Grove but what he invented.
Now in a house of his own, working,
there is green growing on his roots.
He speculates whether or not it ever was
as he remembered it.

8.

After morning roll,
the boy abandons
to the middle-distance
of distraction and tramps
at a dreamer's pace as if
he were in an old movie reel
frame after frame trailing off
to mother's railtown poolhall
past the ash grove.
How we remember it back to him,
the boxcars he rode for miles
ambling far as town
and back before dark
and his mother loosed the old dogma
from her glass whistle,
and the vague lilt of French
pidgins from her gullet. Drunk,
the Keeper calls an old man
to fiddle spoons as the boy softshoes
lotus wheels in the sawdust.

9.

Ideally, the ash would be part of the pronouncement
of some sort of final fulfillment for everyone,
and perhaps it is. The woman who knows
she will have to sell the piano
she sits down to play, and once again the child
starts to cry. The old man looks at the ash tree in the yard
and remembers a squirrel's nest. Every day, for one week,
as a child, he had watched over it. His mother leans
forward and lands a stony kiss on his forehead.
He screams awake and his wife turns in bed to look at him.
She sees what the matter is. He walks in the alley
behind the house. Each day is like a light kiss, given
by the country, by its air, its sun, its trees. There still seems
to be no reason to consider him king or god.
Feet tread on the path and the memory is released.
The birds scatter consistent with blood-splatters.
In the morning the tree is nothing in anyone's thoughts.
Contracts are made at the Bourse and on the real estate tables.
Flies bump hopelessly against the window light.
Men in shirtsleeves, in billows of cigarette smoke,
agree, we must demolish the Ash Grove. A dog jumps up,
its paws against the little engineer's white dress.
Her mother is miles away, in a car, driving south.
The old man is there. A sitter comes down
and carries the sleeping child back upstairs.

Requisition

Maybe it's like the double helix fix of caffeine and nicotine
unscaffolded along patterns of nights run together
wheeling around your ribs after a few minutes sleep
in the cab of your car in a vacant lot while around you
radial pulsars blink atop Tennessee hills from an abyss
so remote and dark the borders of the self fall away.
The first few nights I worked with him, Chris wore
the ankle monitor hidden under the boot cuff
of his oversized workpants who, under observation,
waded into the endless-seeming months of struggle,
who shrugged off timeclocks and scaled his time
to accommodate the volume of the weight he pushed.
At the bell the race is on: loose pallets rattle against
cinderblock walls, and freezing rain splits petals
on the graded tarmac where trailers line up to unload
and the T.L. radios for *more hands on the line to Push!*
Chris, he pushes for you. Maybe it's the same
any number of warehouses elsewhere, the two
together, pummel and mallet, Chris and his push,
to bring you this chrome-plated toilet brush,
this pumpkin and cognac-scented soy candle,
this matching sheet set, of those who dream now only
in the steel-tooth hum of their sewing machines.
And how the steel rails *sing! sing!* for him
and requisition anything strays too close, as the freight
accrues on-deck. Tomorrow Chris will drive back along
the interstate with the same view of the same anywhere
Americana rest-stops and gas stations and spin out
on an eightball like ashes on an astral wind the coldest
winter night, and the litter of his cigarette butts frozen
on the pavement like bubbles blown in glass
stand outside the vendor door.

Shelter in Place

All night, your waters contend
for these rooms, baring out its hailstone
and winter debris. Swarms of rain deshell redbud flowerets.
Porch-life scenes block on block.
A third of the floodplain is up for sale.
The catalpas hardly legible above the rooftops incline
toward the channel.
Flakes of pitch tumble in the backwash.
Sometimes I wade in barefoot until I erode with the banks.
Sinews of moss leak from my drainpipes
       filmed in cotton foam
              speared with sweetgum burrs in the runoff.
Wreathing the sewer grates leaves dwell mournful.
Yellow primrose doze along the vinyl fence.
Sirens shriek to a donated plot.
Even now, you are being forgotten.

The Restless Hour

She traded him my grandfather's watch
for the reading and a few dollars.
A palmist in camp back from a retreat
praying in the chaparral and cheatgrass
outside Sante Fe or Boulder or El Paso
somewhere, the force of enlightenment
he previsioned he couldn't say as if out of
a chemical dream dark and royal
as the constellations of the night sky
on the dial face. He leans his fluent ear
to the spring, an obscure light mirrored
in its bezel. The gears still purr after
twenty years, carries a countless tic,
resonant along its steel holding the cold
arithmetic in its balance.
After, there was fire enough to cook
and heat the cabin. She has kerosene enough
to last the week. Striking a match in the car,
the wick catches our reflection echoing
off the side window. But today is special.
Morning we eat drive-thru
in the front seat of Gran's wagon.
How we measure the same rain
most of the winter except when it freezes,
then especially, when it doesn't rain at all.

Candela

At 3AM sometimes he found the old man
sitting bleached in the static from the lamp of the TV.
There are no names for the colors, the man said,
the first time he spoke to him, *outside*
the visual spectrum. What is orange
but a conspiracy of resolution?
A memory now dry as faded ink.
Mystery of the ocular vehicle found that,
he told me, *vision is nothing but a trick*
of the eye. A radiance absorbed or deflected
off the surface of a thing, a photon forged
in the sun's core travels hundreds of thousands
of years to the surface, and eight minutes
to your eye it collapses. A fraction
of a blink between the old man's voice
and the disremembrance of it. Once,
sometime later, sitting in stained-glass arcade
suffused with light the man's sister came to the service
and showed him the photos she removed
from an albumbook. He watched
a sepia histories, from black and white, washed
in a chemical bath, expose a sharpness of detail,
a variety of color, as the sleeves
were added to and subtracted from.

Differential

Driving early Sunday while
the lights are still up, not past
the frost polished lawns
divided into plots, but graves
behind darkened windows. It's driving
another winter lost to this place,
banking into the patchwork
of sidestreets and shortcuts
racked left to right, back to front,
block on block arranged
in compounding grids beneath
the aurora of hydraulic fumes
hanging still above the city, compactor
grease stained across the grains
of hands, and ears throb still
to the heartbeat of pallet jacks.
In a mantra *day three of eight,
four of eight*, shift. *Five*, shift.
The shift hours accrue time off,
with nothing left over to save.
It's driving nowhere but between
recalcitrant familiars in chiaroscuro,
the old and young, vets and probates
on loan from County. They trade
in the lore of what-it's-like,
the self-same tension fever
turned wildfire finally burns
the breath from your lungs.
Luke home from his second tour
hikes a pantleg to show off
the tooth-sized groove rifled
out of his shinbone. We nod
as if we know that tumult.

We know long nights snagged
on little defeats, knuckles razed
across steel, fractures avulsed,
grizzled hours burned low,
you take the money and run.
5AM winter passes
in liminal twilight, brick millstacks
black against a slatestone sky,
where I left them years ago,
steamheads grazing on stars,
and the asphalt courts behind
the school bask in relief, their nets
sagging and brittle with the first frost
of the new year, or the last.
In an invisible city you may arrive
even accidentally at your destination,
driving home where dull windows
spill parking lot landscapes
and twenty-four-hour motel
panoramas in rain slick neon.

Abeyance

To imagine that time of year
one by one stepping up
to the planks and taking
turns leaping
into abeyance
into the very terror
of not knowing
they were warned
never to take
for granted
                    rising

briefly power enough
to escape up and away
from the oxidized tracks
fitted for cart rails
to the dead parts
of a dead town no train
had sparked in a generation
they know nothing of
and care nothing for
where there is a bridge
                    rising

        high enough
to prove their rite as
warned against as if
positing a question
which is meant to provoke
serious thought
but instead thinks for them
because the question is rhetorical
because it has a clear answer
which is yes of course
as we gave in once too

and leapt for the one thing
we never wanted
and never asked for
          rising

out of nothing
into a weightless spring
out over the blinding tumble
of sky and water and hills
veiled in sizzling silver
vapor to find
conformity comes so easily
jumping
into the terminal vertigo
where for a moment
there is not so much friction
as absence of self
leaving the mind
leaving the body behind
as if suspended
over the river body
          rising

up to meet the body
bending always
to the larger body
meeting the floating shadow
lithe atop the current
the collision
where action perchance
converge and the wafer
disposed to the tongue
of the river
the sacrament of coral and clay
above or below
          rising

High Water

In ice our house this morning
polar cold, fragile
and frigid. The old tomes
grow frozen: the lamp, the plumbing,
the bed sheets and one pillow.
Whitewashed shades stripped
of color and crystalline. Rooftops
conform to arabesque patterns
stacked on an axis of vanishing
perspective where my father's face
swims hesitant above the surface
in every mirror: *you are what you
pretend to be.* Somewhere, I
in middle life absently thumbing
as the wind drives through the drafts
stirs the exhaust from every breath,
tear pages of the paper apart
to feed a fire stove. Some pages
helicopter out the window
and compost in the litter.
Though not all take root, not all bud
brittle figs like tufts of green peach fuzz
that crowns the trim of our house.
Our house that inks rivulets
from windowsills and awnings,
from gutters and drainpipes. Our house,
its capacity for its own impermanence
accumulates in pools imbued
with waterfalls beneath its caves.

My father's conscience is satisfied
with his assurance of the world,
as though calcified, petrified around
the spores of rooms somewhere
adrift the summit of his waking dreams,
and the glacial crawl over our origins
leaves behind only the smallest traces

of ourselves, floating, listlessly,
across a dusting of stars, caught up
in the momentary melee of colors
visible as it collapses through a sheet of ice.
Not the memory of the first
but of the last time remembered.

Yonder Goes the Light

Last Thursday a group met at the no-name bar
after work. A readerboard on your way out of town
in a derelict lot dusted with morning frost at 6AM
reads *smoking allowed beer cold as your ex's heart*
where Billy Gruff and the schoolkids gnash down
through the chainlink to the footpath, down through
the pokeweed and burnt sedge to pick from under stones
crawdads the Cook fried and served with blackened catfish
under the neon Lone Star in the window where
all the third shift vets and Teamsters go after work.
He knows this place more intimately than any other
and it still felt like an alien thing, but he is it
and it is him and has but no other way to know it
of which he is not: *Kick the concrete*
from your boots before you enter. No one complains
about the smoke, roiling woodfire scents rising
in strange geometries. We are many dimensions
occupying the same space answer to many names.
But he likes it for the smoke, for its manners and rituals,
breaking up the continuity, entertaining fatalist fictions
that don't exist or that are hallucinated when his mind wanders.
Shedding, clumps of mud drop off his boots
in a compost of softened wood and leaves that dams
the gutter overflowing and in the middle all bone
and ashwood cleaved from unfinished adobe
by water as cold and biting as rain. A specter leans
out of the smokeworks and whispers: *you attract what you are.*
He'll sleep cocooned in days, acclimate to the climate,
hours pass into nothing and burn on an empty stomach
and regress into a single cell, withdraw into the caveworks
where all maps fail into silence, scaling the graded slate
and wade into the creekbed kicking plumes of black sand
and soot that flame and recede with the current.
When driving fails, and conversation fails, huddled
in the shadowy revisions of smoky neon,
under the corrugated aluminum and clapboard walls
of a shanty hothouse made from the artifacts tangled

in the reeds after the last riverswell,
he remembered coming past this way when he
and his brother ran away from home and that time
had managed to stay gone for days following the rail line
like a couple of infant-tramps chased out of the switchyard
before they reached the edge of town and turned back.

Elegies for Temporary Rooms

*"By that time in my life, I recognized the room was temporary—
from the start, I accepted the dwelling's transitory nature."*
Spencer Reece, "The Upper Room"

Arriving as we are now, the streets
still damp and steaming,
I wondered if you would remember these rooms

for a time, with the upright
in the basement at the children's home on Smith Street,
with the couple who kept horses in the backyard,
and the mason's pink granite clung to us
in winter like snow,

                  and our nurse
led us in cowboy songs and hymns on Sunday night
while counselors accompanied on acoustic
when we sang late and
rose early to catch the bus to school.
               This room

we used to have one just like it
back in the little blue house on Loren
where the twins were born
and the Kimball baby grand stood silent
for Lutheran bells in windows I now pass
every other day to the university.

Those afternoons mother made a breezeway
after she finished playing her set
with beasts and babes who stirred for nothing
wanted for nothing
chased corpuscles of light from a prism
hanging on a string in the window.

I open the door to the stairwell
to let in the neighbor's cats
to whom all the rooms of the world belong

I open the windows to let out the old notes
as only in memory she begins
one cat perched on the lid considering Chopin's
bronze bust
while the other dozes
in a patch of sunlight on the floor underneath.

So You Know What I Think We Should Do?

Since the news flashed your wanted poster,
there you were standing with a stranger
on Redriver, barely glimpsed
as I passed in the opposite direction.

I write, she told him, she didn't know why.
Her confession he took as premeditation.
In her paranoia she thought some weird guy
was tailing her she said resembled a large mantis.
No matter where she goes, what she does,
it follows in the near distance, not far,
but farther. She can hear
her mother calling her name,
but she can't turn around, and
another year passes. The residue of time passing
petrifies the vines and leaves, the rotted
walnut shucks and husks on the awning
crumbling in the nightshade like antimatter
from time recovered, like an island between
desire and lust for summer. But at present,
he is no more than a vagabond bohemian
and the dark house molds on the ruins
of an open cellar. She remembers everything about
that night. There was autumn on the wind.
A moment shared together, they live only
in memories, in the shifting lightning flash,
exist solely and forever in the moment
of her running away from home

trading the trailer on one shelf of hill for another
scattered down the holler, around the creekbed
where the mosquitoes make more and more,
striking out on her own, packing a bag one night
and following the trail out to the interstate
and there into a dangerous liaison and there
found herself in the city, squatting in a house

with two couples and their friends and sleeping
her way around the group, she goes inside another,
veins drain down veins of drains—
The lust. The storm. Masturbating in front of him—
his beard chaffing her thighs, the longing
in the pain of her own orgasm startles hers.
One of the squatters she knows
from the bar downtown, behind the trolley yard
was stabbed in the face and left for dead on the curb
by a man she realizes is stalking her, but she can't
be trusted to believe either are true, but doesn't
for a moment doubt herself. She's a cold rationalist,
she tells herself, just the facts. Metamorphosing
into a dung beetle, Beatles and beatniks
and 1957 hipster cool the circumstances in life
under which she transforms at the street-level her own
worldview. And the dark house molds, the kids spray paint
on the wall which is under protection by local thugs
who may jump her but who stand unresisting,
wielding their arms limply into cuffs as though
she hardly noticed the instances, and the worst
mornings are cold concrete floors and hot windows,
merciless summer heat, and the soul's certainty
that the day will have to be climbed up again,
and that going down again at the end of it
will be like falling, each instant to be negotiated.
Its siren seem eerily detached in the downpour.

William LaPage is a freelance writer, teacher, and the author of the story collection, *The Vague Terrain.* His poetry has been published in *New Note Poetry, Rockvale Review, The Awakenings Review,* among others. Born and raised in the Ozarks, he spent much of his youth growing up in the Rio Grande Valley. He holds an MA from Missouri State University and currently attends the MFA program at the University of Missouri—St. Louis. He lives in St. Louis.

www.ingramcontent.com/pod-product-compliance
Lightning Source LLC
Chambersburg PA
CBHW020223090426
42734CB00008B/1194